# SUCCESSFUL LIVING from A to Z

Jody Ellis

SUNSTONE PRESS
SANTA FE

*Photograph on cover by Carl D. Condit*



Sunstone books may be purchased for educational, business, or sales promotional use.
For information please write: Special Markets Department, Sunstone Press,
P.O. Box 2321, Santa Fe, New Mexico 87504-2321.

---

Library of Congress Cataloging-in-Publication Data:

Ellis, Jody.
[ABCs of successful living]
Successful living from A to Z / by Jody Ellis.
p. cm.
Originally published: The ABCs of successful living, Santa Fe, N.M. : Sunstone Press, 1974.
ISBN: 0-86534-469-8 (alk.paper)
1. Success I. Title.

BJ1611.3.E45 2005
158.1 —dc22

2005049938

---

**WWW.SUNSTONEPRESS.COM**
SUNSTONE PRESS / POST OFFICE BOX 2321 / SANTA FE, NM 87504-2321 /USA
(505) 988-4418 / *ORDERS ONLY* (800) 243-5644 / FAX (505) 988-1025

For Marcia Muth
and the many others who inspired and helped me

# CONTENTS

PREFACE / 11

The importance of this book and what it can do for you. Each individual has the capacity for successful living, but help is often needed in discovering and using that capacity. This book supplies that help.

A IS FOR ALIVE / 12

Being truly alive is the first step in successful living. Don't be satisfied with being half-alive the rest of your days. Be alive to yourself! Be alive to the world in which you live! Be alive to your opportunities!

B IS FOR BELIEVE / 14

Believe in what you know you can be. Believe in what you decide you want to do. Believe in your ultimate and final success. Believe and it is yours!

C IS FOR CONFIDENCE / 16

Confidence is one of the most necessary ingredients in your recipe for success. Have confidence in yourself. Have confidence in your life pattern. Have confidence in what you choose to do. Have confidence that you will be successful.

D IS FOR DAYDREAMS / 19

Don't overlook, negate or minimize your daydreams. There is hidden power in your daydreams. You can try out your ideas first in your mind and then act on them successfully in your life. Let your daydreams be a preview of your real life successes.

E IS FOR EAGERNESS / 22

Keep your eagerness at a high level. Eagerness is a form of energy that can give you that extra needed push. Your success is in proportion to your eagerness.

F IS FOR FAITH / 24

Have faith in yourself and your plans. Don't waver in your faith at any time no matter what happens. Remember that faith is the light shining in darkness.

G IS FOR GIVING / 26

The secret to getting—is giving. Don't hold back on your time or your talents. Give of yourself, but wisely. Give freely! Give willingly!

H IS FOR HEALTH / 28

Everybody wants good health. You want to enjoy good health. Your physical health often depends on your mental or emotional outlook. You can control your emotions, or change your mental attitude. You can have the best physical health that your body allows, in spite of present handicaps.

I IS FOR IMPROVISE / 31

Don't be held back by limitations, either self-imposed or those of others. Learn to improvise. If you can't do something one way, the way you originally planned, do it another way. Adapt what you have for what you need. Many successful ideas and inventions are a result of improvising.

J IS FOR JOY / 34

Joy should be a part of all your activities. Joy is made up of pride, awe, and pleasure. Through joy you experience intense moments of happiness and living. Times of joy heighten your sense of personal identity. Joy will always produce harmony.

K IS FOR KNOWLEDGE / 36

Knowledge is essential for success. There are two areas of knowledge that you should have. One is to have a complete and honest knowledge of yourself and your personality. The other is to know all that you can about what you are trying to accomplish. Knowledge is preparation for success. It is that all-

important step up the ladder toward your desired goal. Knowledge permits you to obtain an honest evaluation of your self—your shortcomings and how to correct them; your abilities and how to utilize them.

L IS FOR LOVE / 38

A life without some form of love is an empty one. An empty life is a wasted life. You, as an individual, instinctively desire love. You cannot buy love; you must earn it. You must love in order to be loved.

M IS FOR MONEY / 40

There is nothing wrong in wanting money. Money is a necessary and desirable commodity in modern life. You can get the money you need by working for it. Your chances of getting money are greater if you have preprogrammed yourself to expect financial success.

N IS FOR NEEDS / 42

Examine your needs carefully. Are they real needs or merely transitory whims? Are they needs in harmony with your plans? Are they really *your* needs or are they needs which someone else has made you think are your own? Your needs and your goals in life are inseparable and interdependent.

O IS FOR OPPORTUNITY / 44

Be alert to opportunity! Opportunity is constantly around you. Your fear of failure may blind you to your opportunities. Be receptive to what you see, hear and think. Listen to others and to your intuitive self. You can surround yourself with multiple opportunities for success.

P IS FOR PRAYER / 46

No matter what your religion, or lack of religion, the power of prayer cannot be overemphasized. Prayer frees your mind. Prayer can make you receptive to new ideas, new attitudes and new opportunities. Prayer often provides the climate for self-confrontation. Prayer helps you sort out details. Prayer leads to problem solving. Prayer should be a first resort, not a last one.

Q IS FOR QUEST / 49

Quest is not an old-fashioned or out-of-date idea. The man or woman with a quest is lifted out of the ordinary humdrum routines of life.

R IS FOR RELAXATION / 51

Relaxation is a part of achieving success. You must learn when and how to relax your mind and body. New ideas will often come into the relaxed mind. Better muscular co-ordination will come to the relaxed body. A change of pace, a time of quietness or a new view will recharge your thinking.

S IS FOR SELF / 54

The most important person in your plan for success is your *self.* You must know and respect the self you are. You must acquire and develop self-esteem. If you do not have confidence in the self that is the guiding force behind all your plans, no one else is going to have confidence in you either.

T IS FOR TIME / 56

Time is one of the great gifts that you have. Do not waste time because it seems so limitless. No one knows the measure or extent of his or her time. Never say that you do not have *time* to achieve what you want. The farthest, most difficult goals can be reached by using small pieces of time. It is not the day that you waste that ultimately defeats you; it is the minutes that you throw away.

U IS FOR UNDERSTANDING / 59

Understanding is learned. You can learn it by listening. You can learn it by putting yourself in another's place. Understanding is the golden rule in action. Understanding is one part of the well-adjusted mature personality.

V IS FOR VICTORY / 62

Victory is something you should always anticipate. Victory or mastery over your problems should be the most logical thing in your life. Victory can be assured by following a program of tested methods that leads to success.

W IS FOR WONDER / 65

Don't lose your sense of wonder! Wonder keeps your mind fresh and your imagination active. A sense of wonder adds interest to your life and to your personality.

X IS FOR X-RAY / 67

Apply the principles of X-ray to your life. Learn and practice self-analysis. Examine your motives. Understand your reasoning and avoid false rationalization. Be sure that you know why you are thinking and doing what you do.

Y IS FOR YOUTHFULNESS / 69

Youthfulness is a condition of mind and spirit, not body. Youthfulness can coexist with maturity. Your chronological age is one thing; your real age can be much less.

Z IS FOR ZEST / 71

Put zest into everything you do. It will add a new dimension and a new flavor to your life. Put zest into your thinking and revitalize your thoughts.

# PREFACE

Although the world has changed greatly since I first wrote the "ABC's" in 1974, there is perhaps even more use now for a helpful guide to personal success. There is always a need for creative thinking and planning. In the increasingly busy world, it is important to have personal energy. In the competitive world, it is wise to discover your own strength and potential ability. In the face of increasing technology, the successful person learns to balance self-discipline and self-realization in order to have a happy, productive life. You have the key to your own creative and successful personality.

This book can show you how to use that key. Why use the ABC method? As children we learn to read by knowing the alphabet. In a sense we are programmed to respond to that orderly learning formula. The text in the book is designed for you as an individual. There is no right or wrong way to use it. Some people have told me that they prefer to go through the book chapter by chapter. Others have found that they got the best results by reading chapters that met their immediate or special needs. However, I still recommend using a notebook in conjunction with the book. The act of physically writing in your notebook brings you face to face with yourself. Finally, think of this book as a handy manual to a better, more fulfilling and enjoyable life.

## A IS FOR ALIVE

# A

Are you really ALIVE? Of course, you will probably reply, I am reading this page, therefore I must be alive. But notice that I say "really" alive. I mean more than a surface attention to living. Yes, you are alive in that sense, for you are a thinking organism. You eat, work, sleep and perform all other necessary functions that living demands. But are you enjoying life? Are you successful as a personality?

Being truly alive is the first step in successful living. It means being alert. It means using all your senses at full capacity. It means using all of your thinking and reasoning abilities, not just a part of them. And it means *all* of the time, not just now and then.

If you were in a race, you would not expect to win by walking. Don't walk through life!

Don't be satisfied with being half-alive the rest of your days. Wake up to yourself, to your surroundings, to your opportunities.

Being alive is being aware of your opportunities. Opportunities are everywhere, but they aren't seen by those who sleep through their lives.

Be alive to yourself. How well do you know yourself? Do you think that you are using your full potential for living? Take a good look at yourself. Measure your aliveness in the following way:

On one page in your Notebook, mark three columns headed: 1. Things I Do; 2. Things I Am Able To Do; 3. Things I Have Always Wanted to Do.

Proceed then to list the appropriate things in each column. Remember, this list is only for you, so do not be afraid or ashamed to be honest.

When you have finished this exercise, examine what you have written in each column. Your list determines the extent of your aliveness. If there are more things in column two than in column one, you are not as alive as you could be. If there are things listed in column three which are not listed in either column one or two, you have not begun to live yet as you should.

What can you do about it? Don't continue to put off doing things because of some vague future hope that your situation will be different. Do the things now. Don't say, "When I have more time," or "When I have more money," or "When I retire."

Do things now! Don't wait to live!

Being alive can give you new eyes to see the world, new ears to hear the world and new strength with which to work your own miracles.

**TODAY** – *Say to yourself, "I AM ALIVE! I AM REALLY ALIVE!" Go through this day as if you were a new arrival in the world. Use all of your senses all of the day. See everything clearly. Listen to all sounds. Feel the vibration of life in your body and your mind. Wake up your mind! Be alert and alive every minute. You'll experience a new day and a new life.*

B

## B IS FOR BELIEVE

The dictionary says that to BELIEVE is "to have confidence in the truth, the existence, or the reliability of something."

There are some important key words in that definition – "confidence," "truth" and "reliability."

When you believe in yourself, you are showing that you *do* have confidence in who and what you are. You know the truth about yourself.

Remember the old saying, "Seeing is believing." Well, every day you have the opportunity to see the positive changes in your personality and your life as a result of your work with this book. You can believe because you can see the results.

Believe in what you know you can be. Believe in what you know you can do. Believe in your ultimate and final success in what you start out to do.

Belief is the opposite of doubt. Not only is it the opposite, it crowds out doubt. There just isn't room in your life for both these feelings at the same time. Doubt weighs you down; belief lifts you up. You are inspired and heartened by belief.

In your Notebook, under the heading BELIEVE–STEP ONE write these quotations:

"To believe your own thought, to believe that what is true for you in your private heart is true for all men–that is genius." (Ralph Waldo Emerson)

"We have only to believe." (Pierre Teilhard De Chardin)

"But it is wisdom to believe the heart." (George Santayana)

"Believe that life *is* worth living, and your belief will help create the fact." (William James)

These quotations are to help you understand and keep in mind the important part believing plays in achieving your goal of successful living.

I think it would help you if you would memorize these quotations. In addition, as you read other books and articles, you will discover what other writers have said on this subject. You may want to add other quotations to this page.

Now, on the next page in your Notebook, write BELIEVE–STEP TWO. On this page list those things in which you now believe. List your beliefs about yourself, your capabilities and your future. Put the date after each item.

You will want to add to this list from time to time as you increase knowledge about yourself and your goals.

On the next page, write BELIEVE–STEP THREE. This is where you will list the things, events and characteristics that have passed from the state of mental belief into concrete reality. For example, you may have written under BELIEVE–STEP TWO a statement such as this: "I believe that I can work for and receive a promotion in my job." Now, when you receive that promotion, list that fact under BELIEVE–STEP THREE. You will be amazed at how your list will grow.

**TODAY –** *Say to yourself, "I BELIEVE IN MYSELF." Keep that fact uppermost in your mind. Remind yourself that belief comes before result. Remember that you have only to believe and you will be able to achieve what you want.*

## C IS FOR CONFIDENCE

If you were baking a cake, you wouldn't leave out any of the ingredients. You know that if you did, your cake would be a failure. You can't leave CONFIDENCE out of your recipe for a successful life. In fact, it is one of the most important ingredients.

You must have confidence in yourself. To a great extent, others will estimate their impression of your capabilities by the confidence which you display in yourself.

Do you want success? Do you want a promotion or a new job? Do you want to be elected to that office or chosen for that honor? Of course you do, and a large part of your success will be made possible by the way in which you impress people. If you have confidence in your ability and in your competence, then they will also.

Two people may be equally knowledgeable, but if one displays more self-confidence, then he is the one most often chosen.

If you lack confidence, you can acquire it. First, take an inventory of your past accomplishments; second, consider your present accomplishments; and third, plan your future accomplishments.

Take your Notebook and list your past accomplishments. Don't leave anything out. This is not the time to decide on the relative importance of any item. Just list them.

Your list might include such items as these: winning at bridge or a particularly good golf score; finishing a difficult and tiresome work assignment; accepting and carrying out a family responsibility or making a speech. It might include leading a Sunday school class, painting your house, learning a new skill, or serving on a committee.

As you make your list, try to recapture the feeling of pride and elation you felt when these things were done. Remember the feeling of confidence they gave you. Relive that emotion!

On a second sheet of paper, list those things which you are presently doing which require some skill or special energy from you. This list will include things that you do in connection with your work. It will include homemaking skills. Do you have a hobby or special interest? List your accomplishments in these areas. Don't forget any civic, church or fraternal organization duties. These are accomplishments also.

Now, on a third sheet, list those things which you are planning or hoping to accomplish in the future. This list may include such things as a promotion in your work, learning new job skills, trying out a new idea, studying a foreign language, doing something artistic, taking up a new hobby or sport. There is no limit to what you can plan.

Reading what you have done and what you are doing will give you confidence for the things you intend to do.

Confidence is accepting the challenges of life in a vital and dynamic manner. If you do nothing, risk nothing, you gain nothing. Confidence is built by the act of doing. The more you do, the more confidence you will have, and the more other people will have in you.

Stop focusing on your lacks or shortcomings. Don't be held back by the fear of a possible failure. Choose a life pattern and have confidence in it.

Whenever you feel discouraged or hesitate about doing something, stop and remind yourself of what you have done. Knowing of your past accomplishments assures the success of what you are now doing or planning to do.

**TODAY** – *Say to yourself, "I AM CONFIDENT OF MY SUCCESS!" Go through the day acting out that confidence. Throw your shoulders back, look and walk confidently. In every fiber of your mind and body feel the living presence of confidence in whatever you are doing, planning or thinking.*

# D

## D IS FOR DAYDREAMS

Don't be afraid of DAYDREAMS! Daydreams can be a useful tool to you in achieving your life goals. They are, in a sense, mental exercises that can help you improve your circumstances.

Daydreaming is the way you try out in your mind certain situations or possibilities. It is experimenting. Picture a scientist in his white coat in his laboratory surrounded by the paraphernalia of his profession. Picture also how he works, noting his careful attention to detail as he mixes one experiment after another. Follow him step by step as he plans and as he accomplishes his work. In effect, this is what you are doing when you use daydreaming properly.

Daydreaming is bad for you when you let it replace actions or decisions in your life. Daydreams should precede reality, not take its place.

There are effective ways of using daydreams to enhance your life and to add to your capacity for successful living. I call this *controlled* daydreaming. It is not a waste of time. It is a constructive thought process.

The first step in utilizing your daydreams for advancement is to know what your daydreams are all about. People daydream about all kinds of things, but certain things form the basis for the majority of daydreams. Most daydreams are focused on money, fame, professional or social advancement, travel, romance or acts of heroism with, of course, suitable acclaim and rewards.

To discover the focus in your own daydreams, write down the kinds in your Notebook. Under the heading, I DAYDREAM ABOUT, list the subject matter of your most frequent daydreams. List these subjects in the order of their importance to you. For example, if your favorite daydream is about being very wealthy, write down "money," "plenty of money" or "being wealthy." If your favorite daydream is about a promotion, list that, and so on until you have completed your list.

When your list is finished, look at it in terms of the possibility of actual achievement. Go through the list, mark those daydreams with a "p" if they are at all possible to achieve. Daydreams which are beyond the limits of actual possibility should be marked "f" for fantasy. Do not spend further time on these.

Your daydreams marked "p" are the ones you can use for goal achievement. Examine those daydreams to discover components you can transfer into action. Suppose that your daydream is about a job promotion. In your daydream the change in your status is always sudden and without any great effort on your part. In real life, any promotion you receive is going to require work and effort. No one is going to hand you a promotion; you have to earn it.

Your daydream should be analyzed to see what steps you need to take to achieve the goal – promotion. As though you were running a film in your mind, retard the action to slow motion. See yourself receiving that promotion, but more important, see the ways in which you can get that promotion.

The next step is to put your daydreams into action by doing the things you have tried out mentally. List those steps on a separate page titled STEPS TO DAYDREAM ACHIEVEMENT.

Your daydreams can be and should be an endless source of raw material for you to work with. They should be tied in with your goals of achievement.

**TODAY** – *Say to yourself, "I AM GOING TO START TO TURN MY FAVORITE DAYDREAM INTO REALITY." Start with the first item on your already prepared list of STEPS TO DAYDREAM ACHIEVEMENT. Make your daydream come true through your own effort. Remind yourself – "I can do it!"*

## E IS FOR EAGERNESS

EAGERNESS is very important. Keep your eagerness at a high level. Being eager means being interested in what you are doing. It means that you are going to do a better job.

Eagerness is a form of energy that can give you that extra, needed push. It's like taking a magic pill that gives you pep and a new source of energy.

Haven't you noticed how easy it seems to accomplish the tasks in which you are interested? On the other hand, a task which you dislike or one you are not interested in takes twice as long to complete. Eagerness makes the difference. In the first case, you are eager to do the work and eager to see the results. In the second case, you cannot summon up enough eagerness to give you the necessary energy and strength to see the task through to its completion.

To really be able to harness eagerness as you should, you must know more about your own level of eagerness. You want to and need to find out the relation between your level of eagerness and the various tasks, duties and actions in your daily life. To do this you need to make and eagerness chart.

On the left-hand side of your paper in your Notebook, print the words: HIGH, MEDIUM, LOW. Put the word HIGH at the top, the word LOW toward the bottom and MEDIUM in between. Leave enough room at the bottom of the page to print names of the various activities you regularly engage in. For example, your chart might look like this:

HIGH

MEDIUM

LOW

*Job* *Club Work* *Home Chores* *Art Work*

Next, draw double vertical lines on the chart above each activity, indicating your level of eagerness. Going back to our original example, we might see something like this:

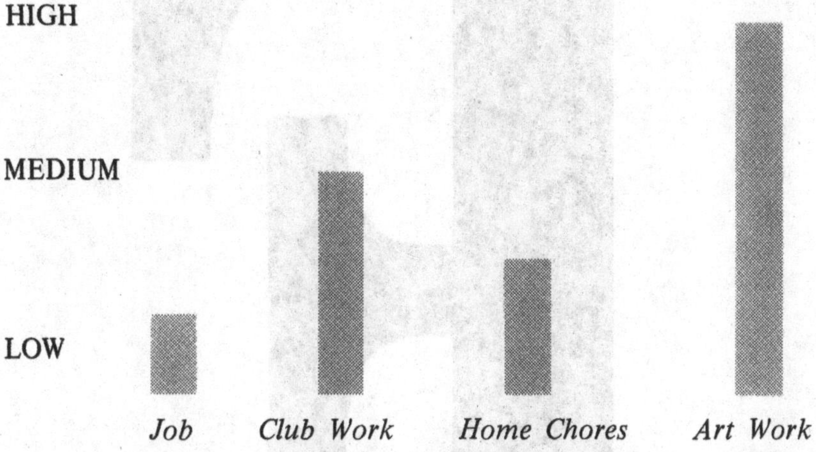


This chart gives you a quick and accurate picture of your eagerness levels. The next step, of course, is to raise the low levels, or to change your activities so that you do not waste time on low eagerness projects. For instance, had the sample chart been that of a woman working outside the home in an office, she might want to consider at least two major changes. Since her eagerness level was so low in housework, she could hire domestic help to take care of those chores. Her eagerness level was high in art work, but only medium in her job, so it might prove more feasible for her to find a job in which she could use her art training.

As always, the important thing is to use the information that you discover about yourself to improve your chances for success.

You must also make a conscious effort to raise your level of eagerness. Keep in mind that your *success* is in proportion to your *eagerness.*

**TODAY –** *Say to yourself, "I WILL STAY AT A HIGH LEVEL OF EAGERNESS." Go through the day feeling full of enthusiasm for everything that you do. Be eager to start a job and eager to complete it.*

## F IS FOR FAITH

FAITH is one of those important but nebulous qualities that can make the difference between success and failure in lives. It can make that difference in *your* life.

Sir William Osler, the famed physician, said, "Nothing in life is more wonderful than faith – the one great moving force which we can neither weigh in the balance nor test in the crucible."

It is that "wonderful" quality that makes faith so valuable to you. Faith gives you strength and a sense of deep-seated power.

In your Notebook, write the word FAITH in large block letters. Keep this word fixed firmly in your consciousness.

First, have faith in yourself as a person. Know that you have integrity as an individual and that you have importance as a person. Believe in that person who is yourself. Keep FAITH with yourself.

Second, have faith in your own plans. Know that the things you have planned are aimed toward successful completion.

Third, hang onto that faith! Don't waver in your faith at any time, no matter what happens. Don't give up your faith at the slightest hint of discouragement. Don't lose faith because of momentary setbacks.

In playing golf, the professionals say that you must keep your eye on the ball if you want to be a good player. Faith is like that ball. You must keep your eye on it to the exclusion of all other distractions.

Faith is what you need for the long haul. No goals are accomplished at once, but if you have chosen your goals wisely, you will be able to have faith in them. This faith will give you the patience and endurance to do all the work necessary to accomplish your desired goal.

There is another way of thinking of faith – think of it as a light shining in the darkness. Faith in that connotation can light your path so that you know where you are going.

**TODAY** – *Say to yourself, "I HAVE FAITH. I HAVE FAITH IN MYSELF. I HAVE FAITH IN MY PLANS." Now put that faith to work in your daily life. If you are troubled by doubts, feelings of confusion or insecurity in what you are doing, remind yourself of that word FAITH. Replace these feelings with faith.*

G

## G IS FOR GIVING

The secret to getting is GIVING. It's as simple as that six word sentence! The problem is that most people are too concerned with the first "G" in that sentence – the "getting" – to understand the importance of the second "G," the "giving." That second "G" word is the whole key to the situation.

You get in proportion to what you give. There is a direct and dramatic balance between those two actions.

Giving is like opening the door and opening it wide so that all kinds of good things can enter into your life.

You can and must put this idea of giving into practice in your own daily life. Don't hold back on your time or your talents. Give!

Many people think of giving only in terms of money or some other material object. Yes, these are forms of giving and there are times when you need to give of your material substance to aid others. But giving encompasses more than these material things.

Giving means *you* personally. Giving means becoming involved. Giving means time, service, consideration and interest.

One young woman I know gives a certain proportion of her time each week to visit the aged in a nursing home. She gives time and consideration; she gets back a sense of warmth and personal worth that enables her to function more successfully in the other areas of her life.

Give of yourself but give wisely. Look for the ways in which you can give away some of the time or talents that you have. Don't give where it is not needed or wanted.

Give freely! Give willingly! No one enjoys receiving anything that has a string attached. And the giver isn't really going to be happy either when he has to attach conditions to his giving.

To make giving a part of your daily life, keep a record in your Notebook of the ways you have discovered to implement giving in your life. Under the heading GIVING write the date and then list what you have done that day that was giving in nature.

Now, for your own satisfaction, on another sheet of paper put the heading GETTING. And under that heading list any unexpected things that have come to you since you started your giving program. You may also want to put the date when those things happened. Remember that, while some of the things you get may be material, such as more money or some physical object, other times what you will get will be intangible – but just as valuable. You may get ideas that will help you to achieve greater success and monetary rewards. You may make meaningful contacts with other people. You will certainly be able to have a frame of mind that through giving to others becomes very receptive to all that is good in life.

Remember, you get in proportion to what you give.

**TODAY** – *Say to yourself, "I AM GOING TO BE A GIVER." Next, look for ways in which you can give. Remember that giving may sometimes mean money or goods, but more often it will mean giving time, consideration and help to others.*

# H IS FOR HEALTH

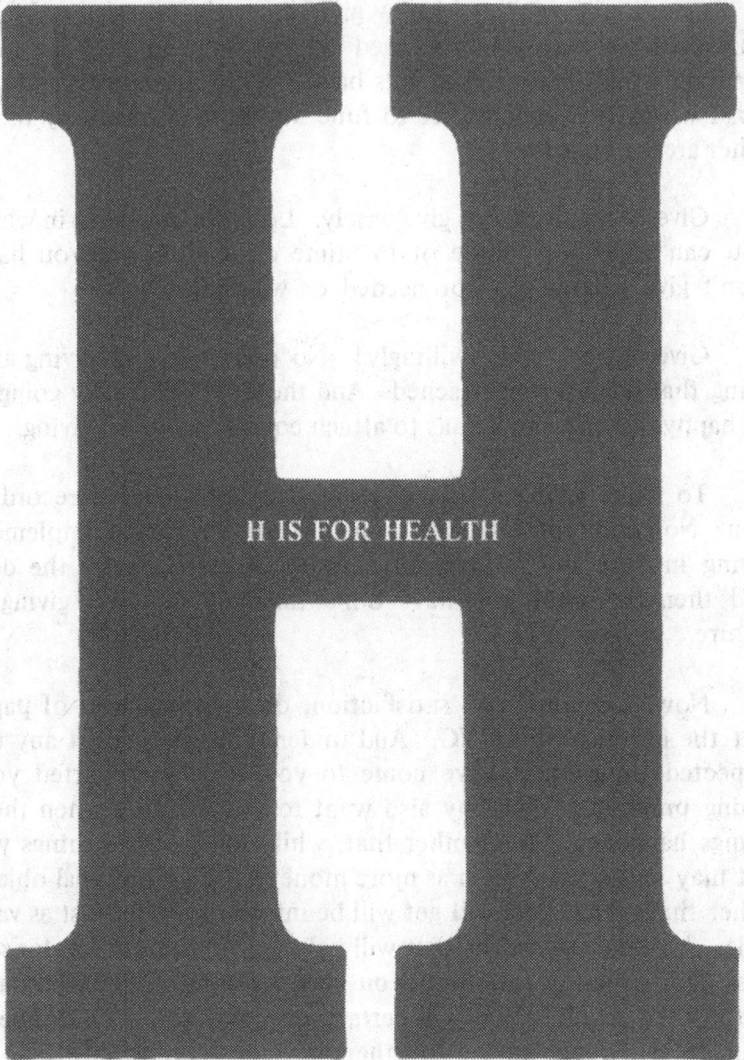

Everyone wants good HEALTH. You want to enjoy good health. When you don't feel well, you can't do your best work. When you don't feel well, you don't look your best. You can't think logically when you are bothered by a headache, indigestion or some other nagging pain or discomfort. The pain or discomfort takes over your entire mind.

Did you know that eighty percent of the average ills that people suffer are psychosomatic in origin? *Psychosomatic* means a physical disorder that is caused or influenced by the emotions. It comes from the Greek words "psyche" (the mind) and "soma" (the body). It is used to describe conditions of poor health which have their origin in the mind or emotions.

How many of your health problems are psychosomatic? Now don't misunderstand – this does not mean that you do not feel the pain or that you do not actually experience the other effects of illness. What it does mean is that you may have health problems which can be traced to emotional reasons rather than to organic or physical causes.

To help you analyze your personal health problems, this is what I suggest. Take your Notebook and sit down in some quiet place. Write the heading HEALTH on a sheet of paper. Now list any recurring or persistent health problems that you might have. Your list might look like this:

HEADACHES

INDIGESTION

INSOMNIA

Once you have made your list, take each item by itself and analyze it in these terms. First, how long have you had this particular health problem? Second, when does it occur? And third, what seems to be the immediate cause? By writing your answers down and studying them, you are going to be able to discover how to solve the problem.

For example, one man who had chronic indigestion discovered that there was a definite pattern to this condition. Although he thought of himself as suffering constantly from indigestion, his analysis revealed that this was not the case. In reality, he had indigestion only after his noon lunch and only on the days he worked. The indigestion had started when he was given a new assignment to a different department. The immediate cause was a late morning conference each day with his department head regarding the work being done. He realized that he had two alternatives: change jobs or persuade his boss to change the time of the daily conferences. After careful thought, he decided that he did not really like his new work and would be happier doing other work. He was able to request and receive an assignment to another department. When this happened, his indigestion stopped.

You can solve your health problems in the same way. But you will have to make the effort to first find the cause and then take the necessary action to change the situation.

Your physical health often depends upon your emotional and mental outlook. *You* can control your emotions. *You* can change your mental attitude.

Yes, there are times when you may suffer from an organic illness, but your chances of a quick recovery are better if you have this positive attitude toward your health.

You can have the best physical health that your body allows. It is up to you!

**TODAY** – *Say to yourself, "I HAVE PERFECT HEALTH." As you go through the day, do not allow yourself to succumb to feelings of ill health. Dismiss these thoughts and feelings as you would disperse gnats. And, when anyone asks how you are, tell them that you have never felt better!*

## I IS FOR IMPROVISE

If there is one disservice that modern life has done for us, it has probably been to stunt or limit our ability to IMPROVISE.

To improvise means to do or produce a thing extemporaneously. It is to contrive or invent from what is avilable. It requires courage and imagination.

Don't be held back by limitations, either of others or those which are self-imposed. Don't be held back by lacks. Don't recognize either limitations or lacks. Always know that there are solutions to problems. Also, always remember that there is more than one way to do a thing and, in fact, often there is a variety of ways.

Learn to improvise. Don't lock yourself into a rigid pattern of action. If you can't do something one way (the way you originally planned), do it another way. Adapt what you have for what you need.

To successfully improvise, you need to free your mind from any preconceived notions about what has to be done. Look for alternative ways.

If you were on an automobile trip and needed to go from Chicago to San Francisco, you would plan a certain route. If, however, after starting, you found your route closed or blocked, you would not give up and return home. No, you would look for some other route, even if it meant more miles and more time. In this case your goal of reaching San Francisco is uppermost in your mind and you do not care what routes you have to take to get there.

The same principle applies in all situations. When you find your way blocked, don't give up – look for another way. And, if that particular way doesn't prove feasible, look for a second, a third or as many ways as needed until you are able to find the right one.

To help you in this process of improvisation, I suggest that you work out your plans on paper first. This can save you time, energy and materials.

Under the heading IMPROVISE, write your ultimate aim or goal. Next, list the steps you had expected to take to achieve that goal. Those steps may include a method of working, a list of needed materials, a plan of action, or a combination of all three. Mark those items which you cannot do or cannot get.

Make a second list which contains substitute actions or materials. Will these work? If not, make another list. Continue working your plan of improvisation out on paper until you have found a viable plan to put into action.

Many successful ideas and inventions are a result of improvisation. They show what can happen when individuals refuse to be stopped by what appears to be a blockade.

**TODAY** – *Say to yourself, "I WILL IMPROVISE WHENEVER AND WHEREVER NEEDED." Go through the day knowing that you are capable of controlling each situation through your ability to improvise.*

## J IS FOR JOY

JOY is one of the great positive emotions in life. William Wordsworth wrote of the "deep power of joy," and Yeats wrote that "joy is wisdom."

Joy has always been considered a source of strength and wisdom. The person who "walks in joy" walks in glory. He is surrounded by the aura of success.

Joy is made up of pride, awe and pleasure. You have pride in who you are and what you are, which makes you feel joyous. You have a sense of awe at the wonders of this world. This gives you joy because you are a participant in those wonders. You have a feeling of pleasure in your life and this gives you joy.

While joy should be a foundation stone of your life, there will be times when it will be more noticeable. Through joy you will experience intense moments of happiness and living. All of your senses will be sharpened. The emotions and sensations that you receive will be greater.

When you feel joyful, you see life differently. There is no room for disappointment in your life. There is no room for failure. There are no wasted hours of unhappiness.

Being filled with joy also means having a deepened sense of appreciation for all of your varied experiences. Times of joy heighten your sense of personal identity. You know from your own experience that it is more fun to be with a happy, joyful person. The same applies to yourself. You will like yourself better if you are filled with joy.

To help you develop joy in your life, you will want to know what gives you joy. Perhaps you have never thought about it before, but now is a good time to start.

Under the heading JOY in your Notebook, list those things and experiences which give you joy. These might include listening to a certain kind of music, walking in the country, baking bread or working with wood. Joy is a very personal matter.

**TODAY** – *Say to yourself, "I AM GOING TO FILL MY LIFE WITH JOY." Then go through the day consciously looking for ways in which you can experience joy.*

K

## K IS FOR KNOWLEDGE

KNOWLEDGE is essential for success. Aristotle said, "All men by nature desire knowledge." However, you must make an effort to acquire knowledge. How many times have you heard someone say, "I wish I knew more about ––––––." Perhaps you have even said it yourself.

So this innate desire for knowledge is only one small part of the picture. The larger part is the actual gaining of knowledge.

There are two areas of knowledge that you should have. One is to have a complete and honest knowledge of yourself and your personality. The other is to know all that you can about what you are trying to accomplish.

Under S (as well as under X) you will learn the various techniques for self-knowledge. Knowing the "ins and outs" of your own personality will help you deal with the world at large. Your universe begins with you.

Once you have established your goals, you need to acquire all the information and knowledge that you can about how to accomplish those goals.

The acquisition of knowledge should not be confined to those years of your life when you are in school. No, the acquisition of knowledge is a lifelong process.

How do you get knowledge? You get it by reading, by study, by attending classes, by listening to others and by working in a practical way at what you want to achieve.

Knowledge is preparation for success. It is that all-important step up the ladder toward your desired goal.

Make a plan of knowledge. In your Notebook under KNOWLEDGE, write the goal (or goals) that you have in mind. Under each, list the knowledge that you need to acquire to achieve that goal. If you want a promotion in your work, you may decide that you need to attend some night classes in that subject. Knowledge is always available. It is all around you. Why not take advantage of this fact? You can increase your knowledge and win success, or you can remain as you are and never achieve your goals. But being successful is not only more desirable, it is greatly more rewarding in practical ways.

**TODAY** – *Say to yourself, "I WILL WORK ON A PLAN FOR INCREASED KNOWLEDGE." Go through the day taking the steps necessary to get this needed knowledge. Enroll in a class or get a book on the subject you need or make arrangements to consult another person who has access to the knowledge you need.*

## L IS FOR LOVE

LOVE is a basic necessity in your life. A life without some form of love is an empty one. An empty life is a wasted life. You don't need to have that kind of an existence.

You are literally surrounded by love – we all are, but we may not always recognize it because of a tendency to focus on the negative aspects of life. However, you can change that habit of thinking.

Imagine yourself completely enveloped in love – love from relatives, love from friends and, yes, love from strangers.

This love we are talking about is the love that expresses itself in unselfish acts, in words, in concern, in appreciation and in sharing.

You, as an individual, instinctively desire love. You want this feeling of being an object of concern to others. You want to feel this warmth of love.

Where there is no feeling of love, there is loneliness and despondency. These are unpleasant and uncomfortable feelings. You do not have to suffer them. Love can take their place.

Do you think that you are loved? Do you love other people? Do you love things? Do you love yourself?

These are all questions that will help you to determine what an important role love plays in your life.

In your Notebook, write the heading LOVE. Divide the page into two sections. In one section write the words, "I Love," and in the second section the words, "I Am Loved By." Now, list under each heading the names of the persons, animals or other objects involved in a love relationship with you.

Don't question the word "objects" too much, for you may find, to your surprise, that if you answer that first question honestly, some objects will be listed. Now there is nothing wrong in loving some activity or inanimate thing, as long as it is not the sole recipient of your love feelings.

Look at the two sections – do they balance? Are you satisfied with them, or do you feel that there should be some changes made?

Love does make a difference in life. But you cannot buy love; you must earn it. You must love in order to be loved. You must be in yourself a lovable person.

Start out by loving yourself. Make yourself into the kind of person that is lovable. Next, extend that love and concern to other people. Be determined to have an attitude of love toward others.

**TODAY –** *Say to yourself, "I AM WORTHY OF LOVE BECAUSE I LOVE." Look for ways in which you can exhibit qualities of love toward others. Use a loving approach in handling various situations. Put love into all your actions and thoughts.*

## M IS FOR MONEY

There is nothing wrong in wanting MONEY. The world today is run by modern economic methods based on a system using money.

The evils that people often associate with money are not evils that come from money itself but from the ways in which people have misused money.

Money is not only necessary, but also desirable. Like all desirable things it must be earned. Having been earned, it then may be exchanged for a variety of goods, services and other special things which will make your life more comfortable, more pleasing and more enjoyable.

Do not think of money in terms of dollars and cents, but in terms of commodities, services and occasions. Think of food, clothing, housing, theater, concerts, vacations, retirement and similar practical matters and desires.

Are you satisfied with the money you have? Are you getting your money's worth in terms of real value to your life?

Here is a simple exercise to help you compute your money power in terms of personal benefit.

In your Notebook write the amount of money that you have to spend in a given period. You may choose, for evaluation purposes, a week or perhaps a month. But, for whatever time limit you select, list what you usually purchase with that money in terms of commodities or goods such as food, clothing, furniture and gasoline. A second list should show what services you purchase. Include such items as laundry, utilities, housing if renting, medical expenses, insurance and taxes. If you are buying your house, you will probably want to put it on your first list. A third list should include money paid or put aside for retirement, vacation, cultural activities and gifts.

Now, make a fourth list of commodities, services and occasions that you would like to exchange your money for if you could. Check off those that you think you will actually be able to have or do in the near future.

Study the four lists. Are you satisfied with what you are presently doing with your money? What about the future?

You can increase your money by increasing your earning capacity. Don't be satisfied to plod along in the same dull routines unless you are satisfied with less.

Break into a larger earning capacity by developing new or latent skills in your work. If you have an idea for a new service, process or product, develop it! Follow through on your ideas.

Your chances of getting money are greater if you have preprogrammed yourself to expect financial success. If you anticipate or fear failure, you will not do a good job in whatever you try. You will be held back by your own timidity and lack of confidence. The financial rewards you get are in proportion to your involvement, interest and participation.

Translate your money into tangible perceptions. Insist to yourself that you have a *right* to earn and use the most that your ability and productivity entitles you to earn. Increase your ability and the level of your productivity and see a rise in your financial level.

**TODAY** – *Say to yourself, "I AM GOING TO EARN MORE MONEY!" Go through this day looking for ways in which you can raise your productivity level. Think of a new method, a better service or an improved product.*

## N IS FOR NEEDS

NEEDS are part of our lives. You always have needs. You started having needs as soon as you were born. Your first needs were very simple, very instinctive. Your needs then were related to survival – needs for food, shelter and warmth. As you grew, your needs became greater, more complex and more sophisticated. True, you never lose your needs for those basic necessities for survival. You do, however, increase the number of needs that you deem necessary for your survival.

Examine your needs carefully. Are they real needs or merely transitory whims? Are these needs necessary for your survival as a person?

There is nothing wrong in having needs which, when satisfied, add to your personal comfort and welfare. The danger lies in overemphasizing certain so-called needs to the exclusion of other desirable goals in your life. A bird in the hand is not necessarily worth two in the bush if acquiring those two is going to mean greater benefits for you in the long run.

Are your needs in harmony with your plans? You know what your plans for the future are and what your goals are. Don't let yourself be sidetracked by foolish or unnecessary needs.

Another question to answer is, are these really *your* needs or are they needs which someone else has made you think are your own? In other words, do you feel you need some material object or achievement just because a neighbor, a friend, a member of your family, or an advertisement has made you think so? To be valid, your needs must come from deep within yourself.

Your needs and your goals must be related to each other in some way. Your needs in life and your goals in life are inseparable and interdependent.

Needs must be satisfied or you will be unhappy and feel frustrated. Therefore, it is important to be sensible and realistic about your needs.

In your Notebook, under the heading NEEDS, write a list of your current needs. Study your list carefully in the light of these questions:

1. Is this need connected to a goal?
2. Is this need necessary for my survival?
3. Is this need more than a passing fancy?
4. Is this need of my own choosing?

If there is any need about which you have to answer "No," put a line through that need in your list. That is not a valid need.

Study your list again for priorities. See if there are some needs which must be taken care of before others can be satisfied. For example, one of your needs is a new car. You need this car because it is the only way you have of getting to and from work and your old car is no longer in good running condition. However, a need which has to come first is the need for additional money. That money can come from a salary increase. The salary increase will come from a job promotion which will come about if you take some advanced training. Your priority list of needs would read like this:

1. Advanced training
2. More money
3. New car

Once you have put your needs into their proper time sequence, you are ready to take the steps necessary to satisfy those needs. Start with one need at a time and concentrate on that one; then go on to the next need on your list.

**TODAY** – *Say to yourself, "MY NEED IS ––––––, AND TODAY I AM GOING TO TAKE THE NECESSARY STEPS TOWARD* SATISFYING *THAT NEED."*

O

## O IS FOR OPPORTUNITY

We all grow up knowing about OPPORTUNITY and knowing the various proverbs and folk sayings associated with this subject. But knowing all these things sometimes makes us careless about opportunity itself.

What is opportunity? It is, according to the dictionary, a favorable or advantageous combination of circumstances. Opportunity – more than being the right person at the right place at the right time – is being *aware* of being the right person at the right place at the right time. It is taking action as a result of that combination of factors.

Be alert to opportunity! Opportunity is constantly around you. It may knock once on a specific issue, but it knocks again and again for various things. However, you can miss opportunity because you are too engrossed in daily routines or are too *timid* to take advantage of the opportunities that come to you.

Opportunity does beckon every day of your life, but you have to be free to follow. You have to be sure of yourself as a person. You cannot respond to opportunity if you are tied down by fears of any kind. You cannot respond if you have an image of yourself that is lacking in self-esteem or self-confidence.

Your fear of failure may blind you to your opportunities. It may be that in the past you failed because of faulty thinking or planning, but that does not mean that failure has to become the normal pattern of your life. If you let your past determine your present and your future, you are seriously handicapping yourself. It is as if you tied your legs together and then tried to compete in a race! Don't do this to yourself!

Look constantly for those important signs of opportunity. Be receptive to what you see and hear. Take note of how these things could affect your life, your work and your future. Listen to others. Very often other people are the means by which you are going to hear of opportunities that you can use.

Listen to yourself. Listen to your own thoughts. You have an intuitive self that is quick to perceive opportunity. Trust it!

You can surround yourself with multiple opportunities for success. You will find that there is a chain reaction, for one opportunity when "followed up" inevitably leads to another one.

Once you have learned of an opportunity, follow through on it, doing whatever is necessary for you to make the best use of this opportunity.

Under the heading OPPORTUNITY in your Notebook, write down various opportunities as they are presented to you. Next, under each opportunity, list the steps you should take. As you accomplish each step, cross it off your list.

**TODAY** – *Say to yourself, "I WILL BE ALERT TO OPPORTUNITY." Go through the day listening and watching for that expected opportunity to present itself.*

## P IS FOR PRAYER

No matter what your religion, or lack of religion, the power of PRAYER cannot be overemphasized. For that is precisely what power is – prayer in action.

Prayer is a technique of getting away from the smallness of your life. It is a way of adding new dimensions to your personality and plans.

Prayer is a mental exercise to stretch the believing portion of your mind. Belief precedes accomplishment. Therefore, the greater your belief, the more your accomplishments can be.

Prayer frees your mind from the petty tyrannies which you have imposed upon it. It can make you receptive to new ideas. It can help you change old or bad attitudes and habits. It can show you the way to new opportunities.

Prayer provides the climate for self-confrontation. This is important, for you must learn to face yourself before you can face others. In the privacy of prayer, you can examine and talk over your problems, your plans, your hopes. There are no limits on how much time you spend at this. There are no taboo subjects. There are no barriers.

You can talk silently or speak aloud. Many persons feel the need to vocalize their prayers. In addition, the following method will prove helpful.

On a page in your Notebook headed PRAYERS, write down those things which you consider objects of concern or prayer. Do not worry about grammatical structure or word usage. Simply write them down as they occur to you. These may be prayers concerned with your own life, prayers concerned with others, or with exterior events.

Having done this, write on another page how you think these prayers can be answered. What events would have to happen? What changes would have to be made? How are you involved?

Prayer requires action. On a third sheet list the action that you need to take to start the answer of your prayers.

For example, let us suppose that you are praying for a change in your work. This you would put on your Prayer List. How can this prayer be answered? You might write down such things as a change of jobs, a promotion or a change of type of occupation. What can you do to set the answer in motion? You can look for another job. You can see if you are qualified for a promotion and if not, learn what you need to do to qualify. Perhaps you will need to take some training courses. You may want to seek vocational guidance from a trained vocational counselor if you are not sure that you have chosen the right job for yourself.

The important thing is that you take a step toward the answering of your prayers.

Prayer leads to problem solving. It helps you step outside of yourself and see your problems objectively.

It always helps to talk things over and in prayer you are, in a sense, talking things over with a higher power. It does not matter what name, if any, that you give that higher power. It does matter that through that act of communication we call prayer, you are increasing your capacity to think and act.

Prayer should be a first resort, not a last one. You need a starter to get yourself going on your plans. Prayer can be that starter.

**TODAY** – *Say to yourself, "MY PRAYERS WILL BE ANSWERED!" Go through this day working on the answer to the most important prayer in your life. Start some course of action that will eventually result in an answer to that prayer.*

Q

## Q IS FOR QUEST

QUEST is a word that you do not hear very much anymore, yet it is a very meaningful word. We tend to associate it with the romanticism of the Middle Ages rather than with modern times. The word "quest" evokes the picture of a knight in full armor riding forth into the world. But a quest is not old-fashioned, nor is it out-of-date.

A quest is the act of seeking or pursuing something. It is a search. This is what you engage in once you have decided on your goal or goals.

The man or woman with a quest is lifted out of the ordinary humdrum routines of life. Having a quest gives meaning and purpose to your life.

Think of yourself as one of those medieval knights who has a quest in life. You have a goal, you have a purpose and a focal point for your efforts.

Going on a quest is not necessarily going on an actual physical journey as the knights did when they started out on a quest. Your quest may be more of an internal journey as you seek the way or ways in which you can reach your goal.

This is what Dag Hammarskjold was thinking of when he wrote these words:

> "The longest journey
> Is the journey inwards
> Of him who has chosen his destiny,
> Who has started upon his quest
> For the source of his being."

Your quest then, whatever your ultimate goal, will also be one of self-discovery. It is inevitable that, as you start on and through your quest, you will enlarge your horizons and your entire body of knowledge.

As I said, having a quest gives you a purpose. You should have a section in your Notebook devoted to notes about your quest. First list your quest as you perceive it and then keep a diary on the progress you are making in your quest.

**TODAY** – *Say to yourself, "I HAVE A QUEST, A PURPOSE IN MY LIFE." Start acting and looking like an individual who has a quest. Keep in your mind that image of the brave knight who could overcome all odds in the pursuit of his quest.* You *can do the same.*

# R

## R IS FOR RELAXATION

RELAXATION is part of your blueprint for success. You do not achieve your goals by working constantly. You achieve success by knowing how to balance your time between work and relaxation.

You must learn how and when to relax your mind and body. For this reason you should choose recreations that provide that needed relaxation for your mind and body. Usually it is wise to choose a hobby, sport or other recreation that is very unlike your work. For instance, if you sit at a desk all day, you should have regular periods of relaxation which are connected with some form of physical exercise. You may want to play golf or tennis, to bowl or hike. Many busy executives relax by swimming. One woman executive I know belongs to a square dance club. The idea is to engage in a physical activity that will help you stretch your muscles and generally keep your body in shape.

In addition, you should have a hobby which is absorbing enough to relax your busy mind. It may be playing some game such as chess. It may be collecting. From antiques to stamps, a collecting hobby can provide many hours of pleasurable relaxation. Your hobby could be in the fields of either the applied or fine arts.

A word of warning – pick some recreation that provides you with the needed relaxation. Don't select an activity or hobby to please someone else. Don't select one that makes you upset. If you find that one recreational choice does not give you the relaxation that you need, try another one.

Take a closer look at the word "recreation". Doesn't it also spell "re-creation"? And that is precisely what it should do for you. You should feel a quickening of your senses and your intellectual capacity after a period of recreation.

How do you spend your leisure time? Do you slump in front of the television set for hours? Now, there is nothing wrong with watching television if you do not use it as an escape or simply as a way to kill time.

To make you aware of how you do spend your leisure time, I suggest that you set up a page in your Notebook headed RELAXATION. On this page, list the ways in which you spent your leisure time during the preceding week. Did you make the right choices? Did you really feel relaxed and refreshed as a result of your choices?

If you had a negative response to any of these questions, then you should change your recreational pattern. Make a second list of things that you think might provide more relaxation. Try them.

There are certain results to be gained from the correct recreation program. New ideas will come into the relaxed mind. Persistent problems have often been dramatically solved during or after some recreation. Better muscular coordination will come to the relaxed body.

The fifteen-minute coffee break has proved that even a brief period of relaxation can mean improved efficiency.

A change of pace, a time of quietness or a new activity will recharge your thinking. Your chances for success will be greatly increased by using your leisure time for creative relaxation.

**TODAY –** *Say to yourself, "I WILL USE MY LEISURE TIME CREATIVELY." Plan ahead for your free time. Make that time work for your benefit.*

S

## S IS FOR SELF

The most important person in your plan for success is SELF. The old adage "know yourself" is very true. Your success starts with *you.*

You must know and respect the self you are. To do this, you have to become acquainted with your real self. Just because you have been living with yourself for so many years does not mean that you know yourself as well as you should.

How do you get to know yourself? You do this through a process that psychologists call self-analysis, but one we can simply call self-conversation. In other words, by talking to yourself (either aloud or silently) you ask and answer certain questions that will help you know yourself better.

Sit down in some quiet spot with your Notebook. I think it will help you to write down the questions and answers under the heading of SELF. A good question to start with is "Who am I?"

Don't be self-conscious. Think of this procedure as a friendly interview with yourself. This is why I suggested that you pick a quiet place where you will not be disturbed by other people or other things.

Take your time. This will take more than one or two sessions. As a matter of fact, you should make it a part of your regular routine, this talking to yourself about yourself and your plans.

Other questions that you will probably want to ask and answer are:

Do I like the person I have become?
What changes, if any, should I make in myself?
What are my plans?
Are my plans compatible with my present personality?

There are many other questions that will come to you once you start this program of self-conversations. And, in many cases, one question or answer will lead to another.

You must acquire and develop self-esteem. The higher your level of self-esteem, the greater your opportunities for success.

Self-esteem comes from self-confidence. If you do not have confidence in the self that is the guiding force behind all your plans, no one else is going to have confidence in you either!

You can raise your self-esteem by reminding yourself of your talents, your achievements and your future possibilities. Don't dwell on past mistakes, failures or instances of poor judgment. Do dwell on the positive aspects of your life and personality.

It is not the magnitude of an achievement that is important; it is the act of achievement itself. Remind yourself of your past successes, your capabilities and your future potential. You know that if you have succeeded just once in your life, the pattern is there for unlimited future successes. Do not hold yourself back by negative thoughts about yourself!

**TODAY** – *Say to yourself, "I KNOW MYSELF. I AM A PERSON OF WORTH. I KNOW I AM SUCCESSFUL IN WHATEVER I DO." Go through this day with your level of self-esteem high. Be fully conscious of your potential as a person. Respond to all situations with self-confidence.*

T

## T IS FOR TIME

TIME is one of the great gifts that you have. You may not think of it as a gift since you are so used to time as a part of your life.

As a subject, time has always interested philosophers and thinkers. Benjamin Franklin in his famous book, *Poor Richard's*

*Almanac*, has this to say about time: "Dost thou love life? Then do not squander time; for that's the stuff life is made of." And "Lost time is never found again." George Savile wrote, "Misspending a man's time is a kind of self-homicide."

Most writers have considered time as precious as money. Theophrastus, the Greek philosopher who died in 278 B.C., said that "Time is the most valuable thing a man can spend." Benjamin Franklin, in another of his books, had this comment for his readers: "Remember that time is money."

And time is valuable because it forms the basic structure of our lives. We live, work and move within this framework of time as naturally as fish swim in water.

Do not waste time because it seems so limitless. This is an illusion. While time itself is infinite and without end, your particular portion of time *is* limited. No one knows the measure or extent of his or her time.

How do you use or spend your time? Have you ever really thought about changing the way you use time?

Make a time study of yourself. In your Notebook under TIME, analyze the way in which you spent the last twenty-four hours. List how many hours you spent sleeping, eating, socializing, reading, watching television, or at other forms of recreation. How many hours did you spend on your job or some work-related project?

When you have listed all of your activities and their time sequences, note how many of those hours were spent in the following categories: creative, non-creative, productive and non-productive.

A social time, for example, might be considered productive if it involved meeting and talking with other people who stimulated your creative thinking. Any time period could be productive if it resulted in some new opportunity for you.

If your favorite recreation is watching television, that is in a non-creative category. But hobbies that require you to make something or do something are creative.

At the end of each twenty-four hour period, you should feel that you have advanced at least a step toward the accomplishment of your ultimate goals.

Looking at your personal time study, are you truly satisfied or would you like to make some changes?

List the changes that you think should be made. Date your time study with the current date. This is so you can make a comparison when you do a time study at a later period. Select one or two of the changes that you want to make and implement them in your next twenty-four hour period. When they have become an integral part of your daily habits, take one or two more changes and put them into operation.

After a month has passed, make another time study and see the improvement in your life. It is a good idea to make time studies at regular intervals. This will keep you alert as to whether or not you are making the best use of your time.

Never say that you do not have time to achieve what you want. The farthest, most difficult goals can be reached by using small pieces of time. I know a woman who wrote a novel in that way. She had a full-time job and kept house as well, but she wrote on her coffee breaks and in whatever time she could find in the evenings and on weekends. In two years she had completed her book. Had she waited until she had "enough" time, her novel would never have been written!

Remember, it is not the day that you waste that ultimately defeats you, it is the minutes that you throw away.

**TODAY** – *Say to yourself, "I AM GOING TO USE ALL OF MY TIME WISELY!" Go through the day thinking of time as a precious commodity which you have in limited supply. Make the most of every minute!*

# U

## U IS FOR UNDERSTANDING

UNDERSTANDING is learned. You are not born with understanding. You have, hopefully, many opportunities to observe it in your life. But understanding develops within you as you grow into maturity.

There are many Biblical references to understanding: "A man of understanding is of an excellent spirit." (Proverbs) "With the ancient is wisdom; and in length of days understanding." (Job) "The spirit of wisdom and understanding." (Isaiah) And, "A wise and understanding heart." (I Kings) These are but some of those references to understanding.

I am sure that you have noticed how often understanding and wisdom are linked. The two do go hand in hand. You are not wise without understanding.

In the beginning of this section I said that understanding came about through learning. How do you learn this precious quality which is so essential to your successful life?

One way to learn is by putting yourself in another's place. We call this "empathy" and it is an ability that you can acquire. To understand others, you need to be able to think as they do. You need to be able to imagine their feelings. You need to be able to anticipate their needs and desires.

You can do all that if you are willing to become receptive to other people. You have to forget your own desires, your own needs, and your own convictions while you mentally associate yourself with another person. You try to become that person for a few moments and see the world through his eyes instead of your own. It is a little like an actor who is studying a character for a part in a play.

The insight you get into other people's needs, motivations and decisions will help you deal more successfully with people and situations.

In a very practical way, understanding can aid you in solving business problems. It can always help you overcome any difficulties that arise in interpersonal relationships.

Another way of learning understanding is through listening. An individual who is always talking rarely acquires much understanding. Understanding is received through the ears!

Listening attentively to others is a way of focusing on them so that you have a clearer understanding of what they are trying to do.

Understanding should not be confined to members of your immediate family, close friends or business associates. This process of understanding should be a continually expanding one. Think of it as the ripples that spread out when you toss a stone into the lake. Your capacity to understand should be great enough to cover every person with whom you come in contact.

Understanding is the golden rule in action.

To help you make understanding a working part of your response to other people, I suggest that you have a section in your Notebook headed UNDERSTANDING. Start by making a list of those people whom you feel you truly understand. Now list some of the ways in which that understanding has helped you in your relationships with them. Have there also been times when a lack of understanding has caused difficulty? What could you have done to change the outcome of this kind of situation?

Make a second list of those other people for whom you should have understanding. List some of the ways in which you can develop the understanding you need.

Always keep in mind what was said above – understanding is the golden rule in action.

**TODAY** – *Say to yourself, "I WILL APPLY UNDERSTANDING IN ALL SITUATIONS." Go through the day making the mental and emotional effort so necessary to understand the people you live with, the people you work with, and the various people with whom you come into contact during this time. See for yourself what a marvelous difference understanding makes!*

# V

## V IS FOR VICTORY

VICTORY is something you should always anticipate. Victory, or mastery over your problems, should be the most logical thing in your life. Victory, or the achievement of your goals, should be the expected result in your life.

General MacArthur said, "In war there is no substitute for victory." We can paraphrase that to say, "In life there is no substitute for victory."

Keep in mind that the ultimate goal of all that you plan and do is victory. You must want to win. Man is a naturally competitive creature. The will to win is inherent in human nature. You should always strive for victory, whether it is in the area of your work or in some hobby.

Victory in your life can take various forms. It can be the victory of getting a desired promotion, or moving up to that better housing you wanted for your family. Victory may mean gaining mastery over your temper. It may mean solving a difficult personal or family situation. Whatever form it takes, any victory is a milestone achievement in your life.

Victory can be assured by following a program of tested methods that leads to success. Victory comes because you take the time in your daily life to apply what you have learned about achieving your goals.

You start with a plan just as a General starts with his outline of military strategy. In your Notebook write the heading, VICTORY COUNTS! Next, take any one goal that you have and want to see achieved. Write the name of that goal at the top of your sheet under the main heading. At the bottom of your sheet, write in capital letters the word VICTORY. Draw two parallel lines from the top heading to the bottom word. Within these lines list the strategy you need to follow to gain victory. Try not to overlook anything.

For example, this is the way your sheet might look if your goal was to learn to play a better game of tennis:

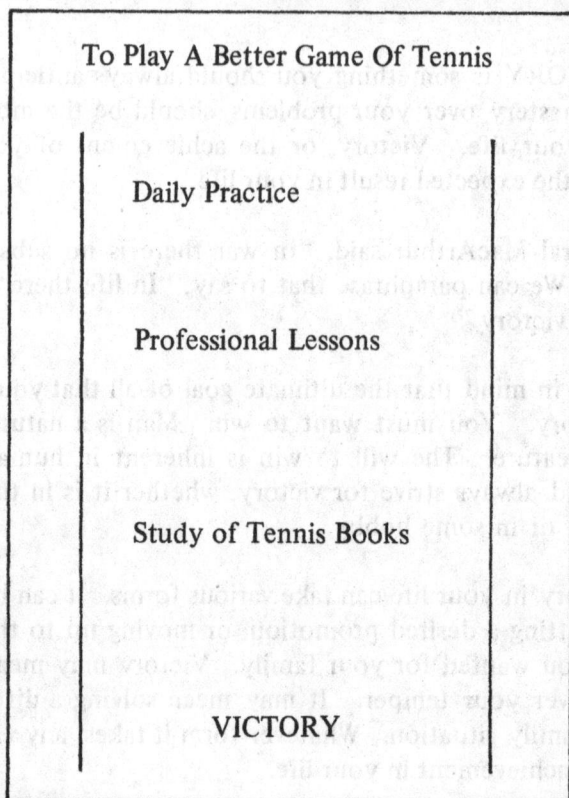

| To Play A Better Game Of Tennis |
|---|
| Daily Practice |
| Professional Lessons |
| Study of Tennis Books |
| VICTORY |

Make out a sheet for each victory that you desire in your life. Then follow the strategy you have planned.

Above all, don't become discouraged. Victory does not come easily. It takes time and effort. You must have patience and persistence. Keep in mind General Marshall's statement, "It is morale that wins the victory."

**TODAY –** *Say to yourself, "I SHALL ACHIEVE VICTORY!" Go through the day as a victorious General would. You know that you have insured your success by preparing a plan of action. Victory is the inevitable result.*

## W IS FOR WONDER

Don't lose your sense of WONDER! Wonder keeps your mind fresh and your imagination active. Wonder is like the yeast that activates the dough.

Children have this marvelous sense of wonder. To them the world is a place of magical discovery – day after day. Unfortunately, too many adults grow up and away from this sense of wonder. They may even deliberately stifle the feeling, having the wrong notion that it is "childish" or immature.

But keeping that sense of wonder and using it to enrich your adult life is really a form of maturity.

Pearl Buck wrote, "I am so absorbed in the wonder of earth and the life upon it that I cannot think of heaven and the angels." And G.K. Chesterton said, "The world will never starve for wonder; but only for want of wonder."

Wonder not only helps you personally, but it also helps you in your relationships with other people. It adds interest to your personality. It makes you more interesting to other people.

Accepting things without question and without wonder means that you are deliberately depriving yourself of a necessary ingredient in your life – the excitement of wonder!

Wonder is the feeling that finds you responding in awe, astonishment, surprise, or admiration. How long has it been since you have felt these particular emotions?

Put wonder back into your life and see your surroundings with new eyes. Wonder will enable you to hear the subtlest of sounds with renewed intensity. Wonder will make it possible for you to taste what you eat with a gourmet's delight even when it is everyday fare.

In your Notebook, write the heading A SENSE OF WONDER. At the end of each day list the things or events that have stimulated your sense of wonder. By noting which types of things cause you to feel that sense of wonder, you can not only increase your sense of wonder, but you can also learn to develop it in other areas. For instance, if you find that your sense of wonder is more often stimulated by visual experience, then you can work on the perceptions that come to you through your other senses. In time your sense of wonder can be stimulated by all that you see, do, hear and participate in, either directly or indirectly.

**TODAY** – *Say to yourself, "I AM GOING TO USE MY SENSE OF WONDER." Go through the day consciously responding to events and people as if the day was an entirely new experience for you.*

X

## X IS FOR X-RAY

We all know what an X-RAY is and what it can do in medical science. X-rays are used to discover disease, to check the process of healing and to assist in healing diseases. You can apply these same principles of X-ray therapy to your own life.

Think of your own mind, your own mental process as a kind of X-ray machine which you can use upon yourself for the purpose of being more successful.

Examine your motives. Turn the X-ray of self-analysis on them. Why do you choose one course of action rather than another? Why do you make one decision rather than another?

You know that sometimes your choices are motivated by emotional reasons rather than practical ones. Envy may be a prompting factor; jealousy or anger may influence the decision you make.

Fear may be the real determining factor in your life. Overconfidence, which can be as disastrous as inhibiting fear, may be the force that motivates you.

You may be cheating yourself of your own success because you do not understand what lies behind your actions. Don't let the wrong reasons determine your life and your future.

Understand your reasoning and avoid false rationalization. You are the one who suffers the most when you make the wrong decision. You are the one who jeopardizes your success when you talk yourself into a wrong decision or course of action.

Be sure that you know why you are thinking and doing what you do. You alone can determine and know your *real* reasons, and your *true* motivations.

The time to apply this X-ray principle to your life is *now*. It doesn't take much extra time to examine your motives. Before you say "yes" or "no" to a question, before you start some action, know why you are behaving and responding in that particular fashion.

A good way to start is by listing your motives behind a decision. In your Notebook under X-RAY write first your decision, then list the reasons why you made that decision. Remember to think of your mind as an X-ray machine that is going to reveal the true picture to you. And, remember also, that a machine can have no prejudice, no tendency toward false rationalization. Be honest about your motivations.

After you have completed your list, cross off any motives which are unreasonable, faulty or unworthy. Watch for those emotional motivations which come from anger, jealousy, envy, hate and other negative responses.

Once you have examined and exposed your motivations, you may want to change your decision.

Knowing *why* you decide can help you make the best decision.

**TODAY** – *Say to yourself, "I AM GOING TO APPLY THE X-RAY THEORY TO MY DECISIONS AND ACTIONS." Then, go through the day doing just that – examining your motives and then acting in a logical way. You will find that you will make better decisions when you turn your mental X-ray on your own thought processes.*

## Y IS FOR YOUTHFULNESS

Being young has always been considered desirable. Yet, there is no way to stop the process of aging. However, you can distinguish between physical aging and mental aging. You can control the aging process by having the right mental attitude.

In reality, YOUTHFULNESS is a condition of mind and spirit, not body. I am sure that you have known young people who already seemed old and aged people who seemed much younger than their actual years.

The secret of youthfulness is *in the mind*. Take out your Notebook and under the heading YOUTHFULNESS list the things that are most associated with advanced age and those we tend to associate with youth. Make two lists – one under AGE, one under YOUTH.

Under AGE you may want to list such things as slowness, poor posture, complaints of poor health, "closed" mind, rigid attitudes, lack of interest in new things, diminished energy, forgetfulness and diminished creativity. You may think of some other qualities. Under YOUTH you might list such qualities as physical energy, good health, creativity, "new" ideas and emotional resilience.

When you have completed your list, put a check mark beside those qualities which you think best describe yourself and your own attitudes. Are you as youthful as you should be? Are you as youthful as you would like to be?

Looking at your list, what things should you start changing? To be youthful, you have to act and feel youthful. It is up to you to decide what age bracket you want to be in. Your chronological age is one thing; your real age can be much less. With qualities of youthfulness in your life, you will find that creativity, success and all the other good things in life will come more easily to you.

Being youthful in your spirit and mind will actually make you look more youthful in appearance. You will find that your friends and family will be favorably impressed by your energy and capability.

There is an advantage to staying youthful when you are older, for you now have the emotional maturity to make the most of your youthful feelings and attitudes. Youthfulness can coexist with maturity. The two qualities in combination give you a winner's personality.

**TODAY –** *Say to yourself, "I AM GOING TO PUT YOUTHFULNESS BACK INTO MY LIFE." Feeling young means having an open mind. It means pulling your shoulders back. It means walking with a bounce. Try it and see the wonderful difference it makes in your life.*

# Z

## Z IS FOR ZEST

ZEST – even the word itself has a positive sound. Try saying it aloud – "Zest!" It also has a good feeling about it, doesn't it?

Some of the dictionary meanings of zest are: "spirited enjoyment," "wholehearted interest," "keen relish" and "hearty pleasure." Well, all of those things would add to your life and thereby increase your chances for success. Who does not want to become wholeheartedly interested and involved in life? We all do and we all should be. *You* can have this wholehearted interest and enjoyment that zest promises.

The secret is to put zest into everything that you do. You know how food is improved when you add seasoning, and how bland and unappetizing it can be without any seasoning. The same holds true for your life. If it seems dull, uneventful and lacking in success, it may be because you don't put any zest into what you do.

Some individuals are enthusiastic about their hobbies. They put zest into all of their leisure hours and recreational activities. That's fine, but they are losing out because they don't have the same zestful attitude toward their work.

Zest will add a new dimension and a new flavor to your life. A machinist who had been bored with his work decided to see what would happen if he changed his attitude. He tackled his day's work with zest. The workday seemed shorter and he found that he felt less tired at the end of his shift. Zest had made it possible for him to enjoy his work.

Put zest into your thinking and revitalize your thoughts. You will find that it is like opening a closed door. Suddenly you see new and better opportunities. That machinist, for example, discovered a better way to handle the product he was working with. His grateful employers gave him a substantial bonus to show their appreciation. Zest brought him success, and it can do the same for you.

In your Notebook under ZEST list those activities which you do with zest. Next list those which you do not feel any zest in doing. Ask yourself if you could not put zest into those same activities. Then try it – say for even one week. After that, write down in your Notebook the changes that have occurred since you put zest into *all* your activities and interests.

**TODAY** – *Say to yourself, "I WILL PUT ZEST INTO ALL OF MY VARIOUS ACTIVITIES." Go through the day filled with enthusiasm and keen interest in all that you do. Don't regard any task as too dull or too uninteresting.*

www.ingramcontent.com/pod-product-compliance
Lightning Source LLC
Chambersburg PA
CBHW010859090426
42738CB00018B/3447
* 9 7 8 0 8 6 5 3 4 4 6 9 3 *